W9-CTX-261

DINOSAUR FACT DIG

ANKYLOSAURUS
AND OTHER ARMORED DINOSAURS
THE NEED-TO-KNOW FACTS

BY
KATHRYN CLAY

Consultant: Mathew J. Wedel, PhD
Associate Professor
Western University of Health Services

CAPSTONE PRESS
a capstone imprint

A+ Books are published by Capstone Press,
1710 Roe Crest Drive, North Mankato, Minnesota 56003
www.mycapstone.com

Library of Congress Cataloging-in-Publication Data
Clay, Kathryn, author.
Ankylosaurus and other armored dinosaurs : the need-to-know facts / by Kathryn Clay.
pages cm. – (A+ books. Dinosaur fact dig)
Audience: Ages 4-8.
Audience: K to grade 3.
Summary: "Full-color images and simple text introduce young readers to different armored
dinosaurs, including their physical characteristics, habitats, and diets"– Provided by publisher.
Includes bibliographical references and index.
ISBN 978-1-4914-9646-6 (library binding)
ISBN 978-1-4914-9653-4 (paperback)
ISBN 978-1-4914-9659-6 (eBook PDF)
1. Ankylosaurus–Juvenile literature. 2. Dinosaurs–Juvenile literature. 3. Armored animals–
Juvenile literature. I. Title.
QE862.O65C524 2016
567.91–dc23   2015028514

EDITORIAL CREDITS:
Michelle Hasselius, editor; Kazuko Collins, designer; Wanda Winch, media researcher;
Gene Bentdahl, production specialist

IMAGE CREDITS: All images by Jon Hughes except: MapArt (maps), Shutterstock: Elena
Elisseeva, green gingko leaf, Jiang Hongyan, yellow gingko leaf, Taigi, paper background

Printed in US.
007535CGS16

**NOTE TO PARENTS, TEACHERS,
AND LIBRARIANS:**
This Dinosaur Fact Dig book uses
full-color images and a nonfiction format
to introduce the concept of armored
dinosaurs. *Ankylosaurus and Other Armored
Dinosaurs* is designed to be read aloud to
a pre-reader or to be read independently
by an early reader. Images help listeners
and early readers understand the text and
concepts discussed. The book encourages
further learning by including the following
sections: Table of Contents, Glossary, Read
More, Internet Sites, Critical Thinking Using
the Common Core, and Index. Early readers
may need assistance using these features.

TABLE OF CONTENTS

Whack! Meat-eating dinosaurs didn't stand a chance against Ankylosaurus and other armored dinosaurs. Many of these giant armored dinosaurs had clubbed tails, which they'd use to strike nearby predators.

These dinosaurs lived between 160 and 65 million years ago. Their bodies were covered in thick armor to protect against enemies. Other armored dinosaurs included the speedy Minmi and the tiny Scutellosaurus. Though different sizes, each found ways to guard against enemies.

ALETOPELTA

PRONOUNCED: uh-LET-o-PEL-ta

NAME MEANING: wandering shield

TIME PERIOD LIVED: Late Cretaceous Period, about 70 million years ago

LENGTH: 16 feet (5 meters)

WEIGHT: 2.2 tons (2 metric tons)

TYPE OF EATER: herbivore

PHYSICAL FEATURES: heavy shields and spikes around shoulders and neck, plates along tail

ALETOPELTA was named in 2001.

Eight ALETOPELTA teeth were found in California.

Aletopelta lived in the mountains of western North America.

N
W · E
S

■ where this dinosaur lived

After **ALETOPELTA** died, its body sank to the sea floor. It formed a tiny reef for ancient clams to live on.

ALETOPELTA had a club tail, like many dinosaurs in this group.

ANKYLOSAURUS

PRONOUNCED: ANG-kuh-lo-SAWR-us

NAME MEANING: fused lizard

TIME PERIOD LIVED: Late Cretaceous Period, about 65 million years ago

LENGTH: 30 feet (9 m)

WEIGHT: 6.5 tons (6 metric tons)

TYPE OF EATER: herbivore

PHYSICAL FEATURES: body covered in armor except for stomach, bony club at the end of tail

ANKYLOSAURUS weighed about as much as a bull elephant today.

Ankylosaurus lived in western North America.

N
W E
S

where this dinosaur lived

A whole **ANKYLOSAURUS** skeleton has never been found.

A model of **ANKYLOSAURUS** was displayed at the 1964 World's Fair.

ANKYLOSAURUS even had armor protecting its eyelids.

8

A full-grown **ANKYLOSAURUS** could swing its club tail hard enough to break bones. The dinosaur's club was made from big tailbones that grew together.

EDMONTONIA

PRONOUNCED: ED-mawn-TOH-nee-uh

NAME MEANING: named for the Edmonton Formation in Alberta, Canada, where its fossils were discovered

TIME PERIOD LIVED: Late Cretaceous Period, about 70 million years ago

LENGTH: 19 feet (6 m)

WEIGHT: 3.3 tons (3 metric tons)

TYPE OF EATER: herbivore

PHYSICAL FEATURES: back covered with armor and large spikes, pointy beak

Three different **EDMONTONIA** species have been found.

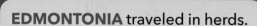

EDMONTONIA traveled in herds.

Edmontonia lived in today's Montana and Alberta, Canada.

where this dinosaur lived

Paleontologists know more about **EDMONTONIA** than other armored dinosaurs because they have found complete skeletons.

EUOPLOCEPHALUS

PRONOUNCED: YOU-oh-plo-SEF-ah-lus

NAME MEANING: well-armored head

TIME PERIOD LIVED: Late Cretaceous Period, about 70 million years ago

LENGTH: 20 feet (6 m)

WEIGHT: 2.2 tons (2 metric tons)

TYPE OF EATER: herbivore

PHYSICAL FEATURES: ring of armor around its neck, club at end of tail

Several nearly complete skeletons of **EUOPLOCEPHALUS** have been found.

EUOPLOCEPHALUS had tiny teeth compared to its giant body. They were about as long as human teeth.

EUOPLOCEPHALUS was named Stereocephalus, but it had to be changed. An insect had the name first.

Euoplocephalus lived in western North America and Alberta, Canada.

N
W E
S

where this dinosaur lived

GASTONIA

PRONOUNCED: gas-TOE-nee-uh

NAME MEANING: named after paleontologist Robert Gaston

TIME PERIOD LIVED: Early Cretaceous Period, about 125 million years ago

LENGTH: 17 feet (5 m)

WEIGHT: 2.1 tons (1.9 metric tons)

TYPE OF EATER: herbivore

PHYSICAL FEATURES: covered with spikes and plates, row of small teeth

GASTONIA was one of the most common dinosaurs of its time.

GASTONIA'S belly was not protected by armor. A predator would have to flip Gastonia over to eat it.

Gastonia lived in western North America, near where Utah is today.

N
W ←✦→ E
S

where this dinosaur lived

GASTONIA is related to the dinosaur Polacanthus.

MINMI

PRONOUNCED: MIN-mee

NAME MEANING: named after Minmi's Crossing in Australia, where its fossils were discovered

TIME PERIOD LIVED: Early Cretaceous Period, about 115 million years ago

LENGTH: 9 feet (3 m)

WEIGHT: 600 pounds (300 kilograms)

TYPE OF EATER: herbivore

PHYSICAL FEATURES: short spikes on hips and tail, hard plates on back and belly

MINMI was faster than other armored dinosaurs.

Minmi lived in what is now Australia.

The name "MINMI" is one of the shortest dinosaur names.

N
W E
S

■ where this dinosaur lived

A nearly complete MINMI skeleton was found in Australia in 1987.

NODOSAURUS

PRONOUNCED: NOH-doe-SAWR-us

NAME MEANING: knobbed lizard

TIME PERIOD LIVED: Cretaceous Period, about 110 million years ago

LENGTH: 13 to 20 feet (4 to 6.1 m)

WEIGHT: 2.8 tons (2.5 metric tons)

TYPE OF EATER: herbivore

PHYSICAL FEATURES: almost completely covered with heavy armor

No complete **NODOSAURUS** fossil has ever been found.

Nodosaurus lived in what is now Wyoming.

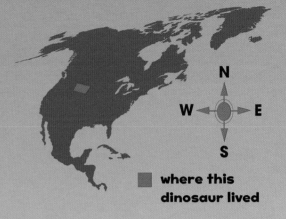

N
W ← → E
S

■ where this dinosaur lived

NODOSAURUS was one of the first armored dinosaurs discovered. Its fossils were found in 1889.

NODOSAURUS was featured in the movie *The Land Before Time 3*. The character's name was Nod.

PAWPAWSAURUS

PRONOUNCED: PAH-pah-SAWR-us

NAME MEANING: pawpaw lizard, fossils found in the Paw Paw Formation in Texas

TIME PERIOD LIVED: Early Cretaceous Period, about 100 years ago

LENGTH: 15 feet (4.5 m)

WEIGHT: 1 ton (0.9 metric ton)

TYPE OF EATER: herbivore

PHYSICAL FEATURES: spikes on its shoulders and back, body covered with armor

PAWPAWSAURUS fossils were discovered in 1992.

Like many armored dinosaurs, **PAWPAWSAURUS** had armored eyelids.

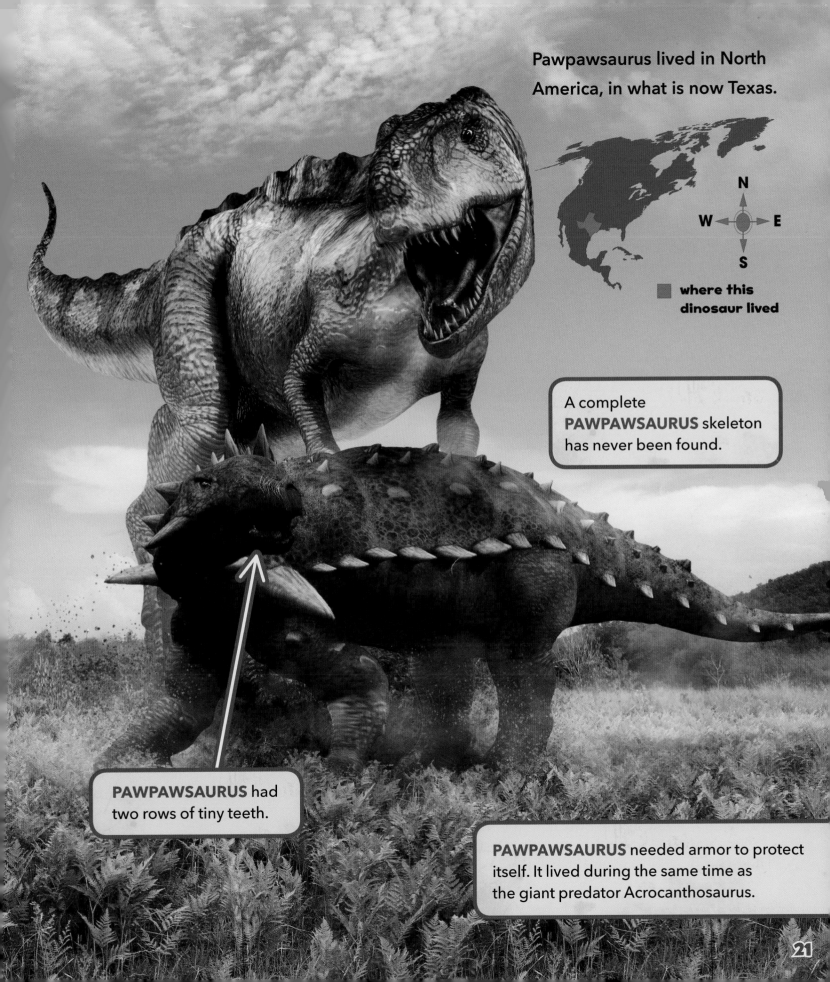

Pawpawsaurus lived in North America, in what is now Texas.

N
W **E**
S

■ **where this dinosaur lived**

A complete **PAWPAWSAURUS** skeleton has never been found.

PAWPAWSAURUS had two rows of tiny teeth.

PAWPAWSAURUS needed armor to protect itself. It lived during the same time as the giant predator Acrocanthosaurus.

POLACANTHUS

PRONOUNCED: POH-luh-KAN-thus

NAME MEANING: many spikes

TIME PERIOD LIVED: Early Cretaceous Period, about 130 million years ago

LENGTH: 17 feet (5 m)

WEIGHT: 1.7 tons (1.5 metric tons)

TYPE OF EATER: herbivore

PHYSICAL FEATURES: hard plates on its tail and hips, sharp spikes on its shoulders

Paleontologists do not know if **POLACANTHUS** had a pointy beak or sharp teeth. This dinosaur's skull has never been found.

Polacanthus lived in parts of western Europe, in what is now southeast England.

where this dinosaur lived

POLACANTHUS is related to Gastonia, another armored dinosaur.

POLACANTHUS walked on four legs.

SCELIDOSAURUS

PRONOUNCED: skel-EYE-doe-SAWR-us

NAME MEANING: limb lizard

TIME PERIOD LIVED: Early Jurassic Period, about 190 million years ago

LENGTH: 13 feet (4 m)

WEIGHT: 595 pounds (270 kg)

TYPE OF EATER: herbivore

PHYSICAL FEATURES: neck, back, and tail covered with horns and plates

SCELIDOSAURUS was one of the first armored dinosaurs.

Paleontologists once thought SCELIDOSAURUS ate fish instead of plants.

Scelidosaurus lived in what is now England.

N
W ← → E
S

where this dinosaur lived

SCELIDOSAURUS fossils were some of the first to be discovered.

25

SCUTELLOSAURUS

PRONOUNCED: skoo-TELL-o-SAWR-us

NAME MEANING: lizard with little shields

TIME PERIOD LIVED: Early Jurassic Period, about 195 million years ago

LENGTH: 3.9 feet (1.2 m)

WEIGHT: 22 pounds (10 kg)

TYPE OF EATER: herbivore

PHYSICAL FEATURES: about the size of a small dog, covered with armor

SCUTELLOSAURUS had more than 300 bony studs in its neck, back, sides, and tail.

Scutellosaurus lived in what is now Arizona.

Two partial **SCUTELLOSAURUS** skeletons have been found.

N
W E
S

where this dinosaur lived

SCUTELLOSAURUS walked on two legs.

STRUTHIOSAURUS

PRONOUNCED: STROO-thee-o-SAWR-us

NAME MEANING: ostrich lizard

TIME PERIOD LIVED: Late Cretaceous Period, about 65 million years ago

LENGTH: 9 feet (3 m)

WEIGHT: 600 pounds (272 kg)

TYPE OF EATER: herbivore

PHYSICAL FEATURES: not much larger than a sheep, covered with armor and spikes

Paleontologists once thought **STRUTHIOSAURUS** was a carnivore.

Struthiosaurus lived in different parts of Europe, in today's Austria, Romania, and France.

STRUTHIOSAURUS and Struthiomimus have similar names. But these dinosaurs were very different. Struthiomimus had a birdlike beak and walked on two legs.

where this dinosaur lived

N
W E
S

STRUTHIOSAURUS was the smallest ankylosaur.

GLOSSARY

ARMOR (AR-mur)—bones, scales, and skin that some animals have on their bodies for protection

BEAK (BEEK)—the hard, pointed part of an animal's mouth

CARNIVORE (KAR-nuh-vor)—an animal that eats only meat

CLUB (KLUHB)—a heavy object often used as a weapon

CRETACEOUS PERIOD (krah-TAY-shus PIHR-ee-uhd)—the third period of the Mesozoic Era; the Cretaceous Period was from 145 to 65 million years ago

FOSSIL (FOSS-uhl)—the remains of an animal or plant from millions of years ago that have turned to rock

HERBIVORE (HUR-buh-vor)—an animal that eats only plants

HERD (HURD)—a group of the same kind of animal that lives and travels together

JURASSIC PERIOD (ju-RASS-ik PIHR-ee-uhd)—the second period of the Mesozoic Era; the Jurassic Period was from 200 to 145 million years ago

MODEL (MOD-uhl)—something that is made to look like a person, animal, or object

PALEONTOLOGIST (pale-ee-uhn-TOL-uh-jist)—a scientist who studies fossils

PLATE (PLAYT)—a flat, bony growth

PREDATOR (PRED-uh-tur)—an animal that hunts other animals for food

PRONOUNCE (proh-NOUNSS)—to say a word in a certain way

SHIELD (SHEELD)—an object that gives protection from harm

SPECIES (SPEE-sheez)—a group of plants or animals that share common characteristics

SPIKE (SPIKE)—a sharp, pointy object; many dinosaurs used bony spikes to defend themselves

CRITICAL THINKING USING THE COMMON CORE

1. Turn to page 8. In your own words, describe what is happening in the picture. (Integration of Knowledge and Ideas)

2. What dinosaur was faster than any other dinosaur in this group? Use the text to help you with your answer. (Key Ideas and Details)

3. At first paleontologists thought Struthiosaurus was a carnivore. What does "carnivore" mean? (Craft and Structure)

READ MORE

Hughes, Catherine D. *First Big Book of Dinosaurs.* National Geographic Little Kids. Washington, D.C.: National Geographic, 2011.

Lee, Sally. *Ankylosaurus.* Little Paleontologist. North Mankato, Minn.: Capstone Press, 2015.

Zoehfeld, Kathleen W. *Dinosaurs.* Washington, D.C.: National Geographic, 2011.

INTERNET SITES

FactHound offers a safe, fun way to find Internet sites related to this book. All of the sites on FactHound have been researched by our staff.

Here's all you do:

Visit *www.facthound.com*

Type in this code: 9781491496466

Super-cool stuff!

Check out projects, games and lots more at **www.capstonekids.com**

INDEX